The Glory of Easter

editor
Maryjane Hooper Tonn

•

managing editor
John H. Hafemeister

Jesus, the Carpenter's Son

Grace Noll Crowell

I can see Him there amid the golden shine
Of fragrant shavings deep about His feet;
A lad who dealt in sturdy oak and pine,
The very air about Him clean and sweet.

*The forest trees were part of all His youth
And something of their strength He made His own;
Noting their swirling grain He learned the truth
Of timber growth, the patience it had shown.*

The hardy tools, the ripping saw and adz,
The plane that bit its smooth way down the length
Of roughened boards somehow became the lad's
Own sinewed muscles with their steel-bright strength.

*'Twas well He worked with wood . . .'twas well He dealt
With hardened steel to earn His daily bread . . .
That shavings clung about Him as He knelt
To pray for grace to meet the days ahead.*

*Painting Opposite
by
Carl Bloch*

The Lilies of the Field

Frances De Planty

"Consider the lilies of the field,
They toil not neither do they spin,"
For nature's care brings beauty rare,
And victories that win.

"Yet even Solomon in all his glory
Was not arrayed like one of these,"
And man must toil and man must spin
To make his specialties.

And the birds, they have no granaries;
Where they fly, we cannot say . . .
But man must learn and man must earn
To reach the higher way.

Then be not over-anxious
For what tomorrow brings,
As man must live in the present,
Find joy in daily things.

Again we see the beauty
Of the lilies of the field,
That do not toil and do not spin,
For heaven makes the yield.

©

My Easter Garden

Laurie E. Dawson

In my garden Easter Day
I see the sunrise with its ray,
Kiss the lilies by the stream . . .
How pure and white the blossoms seem.

I see the dew that bathes the face
Of stately blooms so full of grace,
And listen for the birds to sing
The glory of the risen King.

I see the dawn creep o'er the hill,
And every plant and bird is still,
The sunrise comes with golden ray
To bless my garden Easter Day.

©

For God so loved the world, that he gave his only begotten Son, that whosoever believeth in him should not perish, but have everlasting life.

John 3:16

PAUL MANN

A Stained Glass Window

High above the altar,
The sunlight beaming through,
There is a stained glass window
Of yellow, red, and blue.

It is a thing of beauty
And catches every eye
Of those who stop to worship,
As they are passing by.

Made up of tiny fragments
Which in themselves mean naught,
But when they're placed together
A thing of beauty's wrought.

So in our lives, the fragments
Of tiny deeds we do
Make up a life of beauty
With God's love shining through.

© Katharine Gordon Gabell

Constant Lent

Mabel Long

For Lent, I shall abstain from petty things!
I shall abstain from hate and fear and greed.
I shall abstain from harmful thoughts,
As God has filled my every need.

For Lent, I shall abstain from unkind words
That sear the soul of those I love.
I shall not be discourteous.
As I would wound our God above.

For Lent, I shall abstain from vicious dread.
My homely tasks, I'll gladly do.
I shall abstain from prideful things,
Humbling myself, as God would have me do!

For Lent, I shall abstain from lack of faith
Because I see the faith God has in me.
My heart beats on, whether I'm good or bad . . .
My inner vision now can see!

My Lent, it shall be constant,
For the whole wide world to see!
My life . . . a little less than perfect,
From now . . . through all eternity!

©

Easter Needs

Pearl Carter Phillips

This spring we need the faith that Jesus taught
More surely now than in the ages past;
We need His strength to meet the fierce onslaught
Of madmen who have set the world aghast.

This spring we need the courage Jesus showed
While dying on the cross for others' shame;
We need His wisdom on this war-torn road,
And true compassion for the ones to blame.

This spring, above all others, we should see
The need for more united brotherhood;
We need to map the course in harmony,
And work to salvage all there is of good.

This spring when blossoms tell of life renewed,
We need an understanding gratitude.

Our sincere thanks to the author
whose address we were unable to locate.

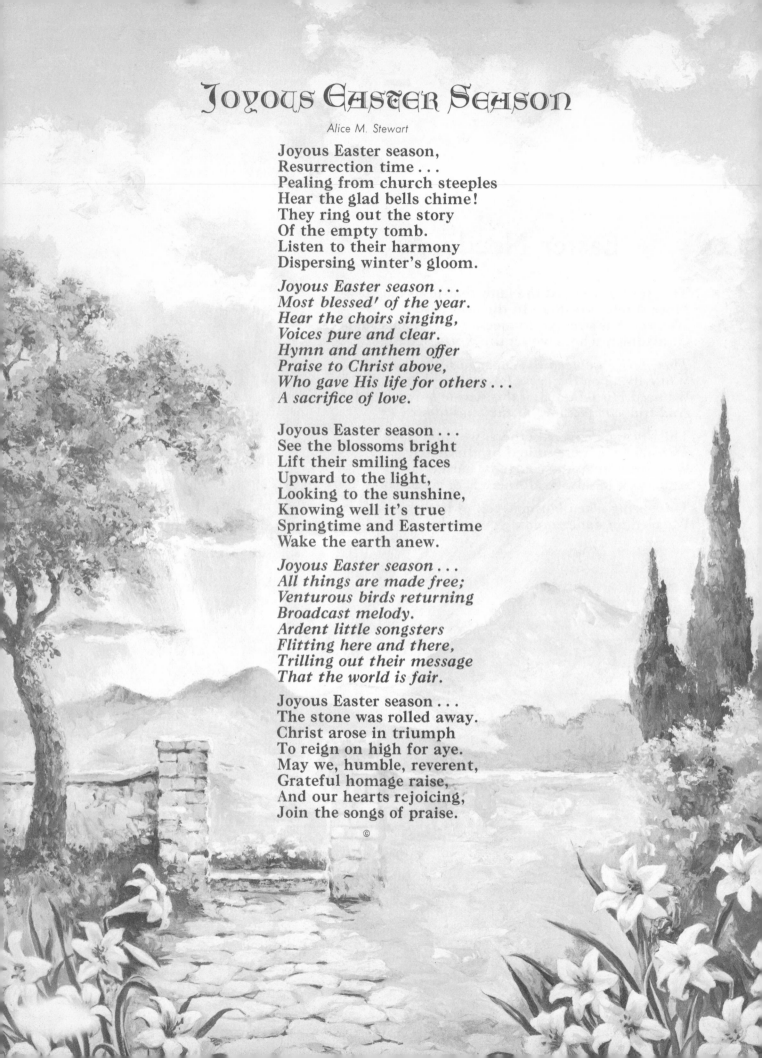

Joyous Easter Season

Alice M. Stewart

Joyous Easter season,
Resurrection time . . .
Pealing from church steeples
Hear the glad bells chime!
They ring out the story
Of the empty tomb.
Listen to their harmony
Dispersing winter's gloom.

Joyous Easter season . . .
Most blessed¹ of the year.
Hear the choirs singing,
Voices pure and clear.
Hymn and anthem offer
Praise to Christ above,
Who gave His life for others . . .
A sacrifice of love.

Joyous Easter season . . .
See the blossoms bright
Lift their smiling faces
Upward to the light,
Looking to the sunshine,
Knowing well it's true
Springtime and Eastertime
Wake the earth anew.

Joyous Easter season . . .
All things are made free;
Venturous birds returning
Broadcast melody.
Ardent little songsters
Flitting here and there,
Trilling out their message
That the world is fair.

Joyous Easter season . . .
The stone was rolled away.
Christ arose in triumph
To reign on high for aye.
May we, humble, reverent,
Grateful homage raise,
And our hearts rejoicing,
Join the songs of praise.

©

Easter Bells

Mamie Ozburn Odum

The night was still before the dawn,
Mystic shadows were softly drawn.
Then came an echoed wave of sound
Encompassing the world around,
And in each heart the music swells
The calling voice of Easter bells.

The sweet tone clings and softly peals;
In reverence the whole world kneels,
The small, the large, the weak, the strong.
Each heart is filled with Easter song
And haste to worship at the swells
Of the golden tones of Easter bells.

And in the roseate golden east
We seek and find a holy tryst.
Here love of God is sought and found,
The grave is naught but garden ground . . .
And lo! the jubilant sweet note tells
The wonder of His Easter bells.

©

Once Again

Marie Elmore Baxter

Once again the Eastertime
Brings the lilies white;
Once again the breezes blow
And the sun is bright.

Gone the snows of yesterday,
Brooks once more can sing.
Bluebirds flit from tree to tree
With their notes of spring.

Once again the church bells chime,
And we cast off gloom
As we worship Him who once
Came from out the tomb.

Once again it's Eastertime
And our praises ring,
As glad anthems we do raise
To our Lord and King.

©

An Easter Hymn

Mabel Clare Thomas

Christ is risen! Hallelujah!
Hark, the mighty chorus rings;
He who conquered death forever
Is today the King of Kings!

Angel voices join the chorus;
Christ is risen! Weep no more!
Every woodland, field and meadow,
Every wave from shore to shore,
Joins with us in adoration;
Christ is King forevermore!

Christ is risen! Hallelujah!
Hark, today the whole world sings;
Hallelujah! Hallelujah!
Christ is risen! King of Kings.

©

Sabbath of the Palm

Edgar A. Guest

This the Sabbath of the palm,
This His last of holy days,
This the glory and the calm
Ere the storm which fear should raise!

*This the day disciples heard,
"Go to where a colt is tied,
If they question say the word,
'Tis the Lord who comes to ride."*

As He neared the happy throng,
Spread their garments in His way,
And with waving palm and song
Greeted Him this Sabbath day.

*Soon should terror-stricken power
Vinegar His cup of balm,
This His last triumphant hour,
Called the Sabbath of the palm.*

Palm Sunday

John T. MacFarland

He is coming! He is coming!

We hear triumphal shouting
from the eager marching throng;
We catch the thrilling music
of the children's lifted song.

The very stones are throbbing
to break into acclaim,
And all the hills exultant
to re-echo back His name.

Break all our fronded branches
and strew them in His way,
Our strength and all our beauty
belong to Him today.

Follow Me

Vivian Hackney

"I am the resurrection;
Follow Me and you shall live.
Follow Me for life eternal."
What greater gift has He to give?

"Follow me!" Have we obeyed Him?
Do we walk in love and light?
Do we let His radiant Spirit
Dispel all the fears of night?

"Follow me!" What peace and comfort
Can be ours day after day,
If we walk in humble service
In the Master-chosen way.

©

Painting Opposite
CHRIST'S ENTRANCE INTO JERUSALEM
by Edward Gebhardt
Stadtiches Museum, Wuppertal

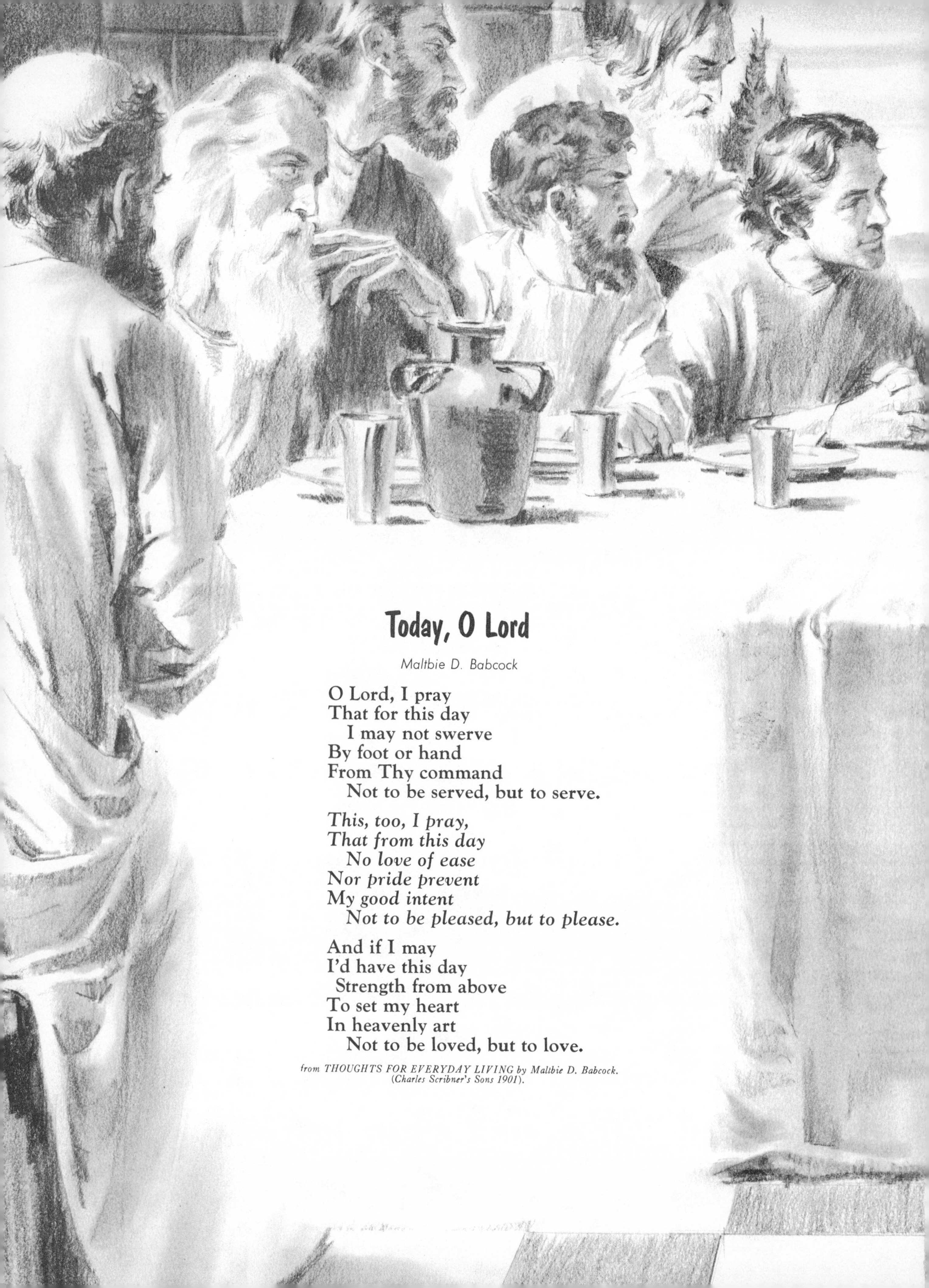

Today, O Lord

Maltbie D. Babcock

O Lord, I pray
That for this day
  I may not swerve
By foot or hand
From Thy command
  Not to be served, but to serve.

This, too, I pray,
That from this day
  No love of ease
Nor pride prevent
My good intent
  Not to be pleased, but to please.

And if I may
I'd have this day
  Strength from above
To set my heart
In heavenly art
  Not to be loved, but to love.

from THOUGHTS FOR EVERYDAY LIVING by Maltbie D. Babcock.
(Charles Scribner's Sons 1901).

The New Commandment

Olive Waldron Warner

When Judas left, the Lord said, "Now the Son
Of man is glorified; with you I stay
A little while, and then I go, where none
May come, but follow after Me, ye may.
A new commandment I give ere I go:
Love one another: for if this ye do,
As My disciples, ye, all men shall know.
Love ye each other, as I have loved you."
Poor eager Peter could not understand:
"Why can I not go with Thee even now?"
He quickly begged, while taking Jesus' hand.
"For Thee will I lay down my life, Lord." "Thou?"
Asked Jesus, "Peter, I say unto thee,
Ere crows the cock, thou wilt deny—thrice—Me."

*Used by permission of the American Baptist Board
of Education and Publication.*

The Last Supper

Dorothy Evelyn Begg

"This bread I break is the last bread
My hands will ever hold;
This wine I drink is the last wine
This cup will ever hold.

"But bread and wine there are to come
Such as you know not of,
Whose mystic crumbs and drops shall hold
My body and My love.

"And when you gather in this room
To take your bread and wine,
Remember it is with Me you sup...
It is with Me you dine!

"Take and eat, this one last time;
This is a holy night,
For Love Divine has cut the loaf
And lit the candlelight."

"This is My body; this is My blood"
So took He bread and wine,
And in remembrance, we observe
This final meal divine.

It came across the centuries
Wherever men should meet,
To speak of One who humbly knelt
And washed His followers' feet.

And then went out into the night
To dark Gethsemane,
Praying, "O Father, if Thou wilt,
Remove this cup from Me."

But history was made that night,
The cup was never gone.
It glows, a holy chalice still
With every Easter dawn!

© Alice Kennelly Roberts

There were twelve disciples
Jesus called to help Him,
Simon Peter, Andrew,
James, his brother John,
Philip, Thomas, Matthew,
James, the son of Alphaeus,
Thaddeus, Simon, Judas
And Bartholomew.

*From an old song, used
to teach young children
the names of all the disciples.*

John Walter

The Warnings

Sara Henderson Hay

These hands are shaped like God's and so
Let them be careful what they do.

Let them be quick to lift the weak,
Let them be kind as they are strong.
Let them defend the silent meek
Against the many-languaged wrong.

These hands are shaped like God's. Be sure
They bear the mark of no man's pain
Who asked for their help to make secure
His little roof . . . and asked in vain.

These hands are shaped like God's. Take care
They catch the sparrow hurled from air.

Lest God look down from heaven and see
What things are wrought beneath the sun
By us, His images, and be
Ashamed of what His hands have done.

In the image of God created he him.
Genesis 1:27

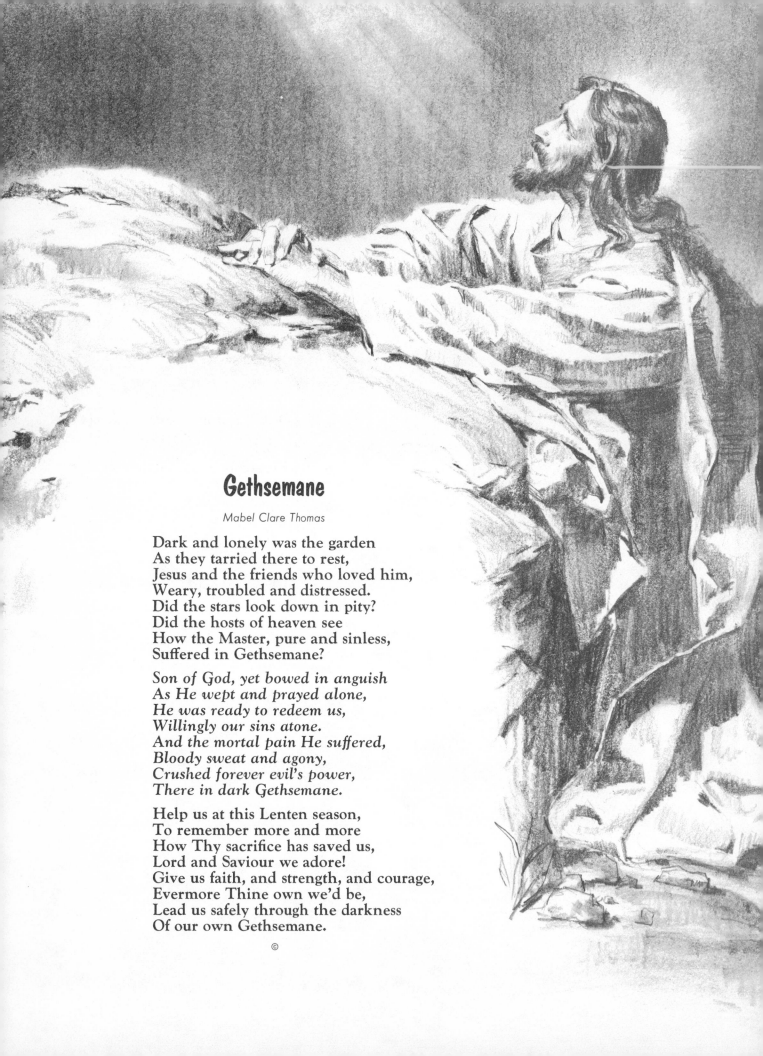

Gethsemane

Mabel Clare Thomas

Dark and lonely was the garden
As they tarried there to rest,
Jesus and the friends who loved him,
Weary, troubled and distressed.
Did the stars look down in pity?
Did the hosts of heaven see
How the Master, pure and sinless,
Suffered in Gethsemane?

*Son of God, yet bowed in anguish
As He wept and prayed alone,
He was ready to redeem us,
Willingly our sins atone.
And the mortal pain He suffered,
Bloody sweat and agony,
Crushed forever evil's power,
There in dark Gethsemane.*

Help us at this Lenten season,
To remember more and more
How Thy sacrifice has saved us,
Lord and Saviour we adore!
Give us faith, and strength, and courage,
Evermore Thine own we'd be,
Lead us safely through the darkness
Of our own Gethsemane.

Remember

Author Unknown

Whenever you know a desolate hour
And are steeped in misery,
Remember Christ was lonely too,
In bleak Gethsemane;
Whenever you feel that all of the world
Has turned its back on you,
Remember that Christ knew what it was
To feel abandoned too.

Whenever you feel that your burden
Is greater than you can bear,
Remember He too heartbreakingly knew
A moment of dark despair;
And remembering these things just bear in mind
His victory was finally won
When He bowed His head and humbly said,
"But Thy will, not Mine, be done!"

Thirty Pieces

Margaret Rorke

Oh, what did thirty pieces buy?
They bought the cry of
"Crucify",
The profit from a kiss.
They bought a trial that mocked
its name.
They bought each false and
fear-filled claim
And Pilate's cowardice.

*Those bits of silver bought
the nails,
The cross, the crown, the
human wails,
The vinegar and gall.
They bought release for one
who killed
So blood untainted might
be spilled . . .
They bought it all.*

Those little coins bought
death for two,
Our Lord and him who was
untrue.
They were a princely price.
They bought for a repenting
thief
Whose dying gasp was of
belief,
A life in paradise.

*They bought the veil
that darkened day.
They bought the empty
tomb's dismay
And Christianity.
Oh, what are thirty pieces worth?
The shame and glory of the earth
For all eternity.*

©

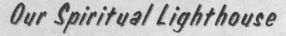

Our Spiritual Lighthouse

Marcella I. Silberstorf

Our faith is a lighthouse, not just a portal
    in a storm,
But a steady beam by life to be lived,
    in any form.
It guides and leads us; when the world darkens,
    it stands firm,
Illumines all the corners as it does
    brightly burn.

*We must build it carefully with a foundation
    of trust,
So it will never topple in any storm we
    are thrust.
The lens we must keep polished, for they are
    the windows of our soul.
With all our trust in God our being will be
    kept whole.*

This beacon that searches within us can bring
    a great calm,
Its guidance brings peace and hope is
    its balm.
May this light shine in our life, without
    and within,
As we strive against life's battles, we are always
    sure to win.

©

The Strong Hand

Alma E. Popazivanov

When Jesus stayed behind to pray upon the mountainside,
He sent His followers ahead across the sea to ride.
The ship was storm tossed, waves were high; the evening
   turned to night,
And they within the vessel's bow could not contain
   their fright.

They feared the vessel would go down; that they within
   would lose
Their lives. They wailed in anguish that the angry sea
   did choose
To threaten them. They looked for Jesus but He was
   not there.
They were alone . . . the Master gone . . . did He not know
   or care?

Then lo, upon the water rough, a form appeared to be;
'Twas Jesus walking out to them in calm serenity.
He spoke and said, "Be of good cheer; 'tis I,
   be not afraid."
They thinking Him a spirit bold, believed that He
   would fade.

And Peter cried, "If it be Thou, may I walk out to Thee?"
The Lord held out His hand and Peter walked upon the sea!
The wind was strong, his faith was weak, his fear he
   could not rout,
But Jesus saved him from the sea and asked,
   "Why do you doubt?"

Do we show signs of little faith? Why not give Him
   our trust?
He'll guide us on the sea of life; to do all things
   we must
Confess our faith and nourish it. Through trust we
   will receive
A steadfast faith that knows no bounds, if we will
   but believe.

©

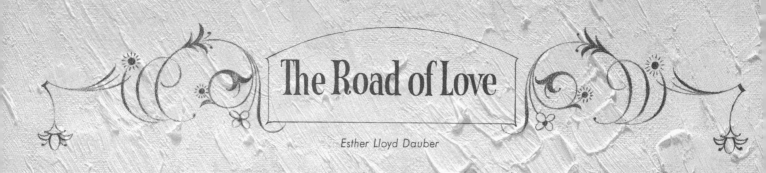

The Road of Love

Esther Lloyd Dauber

From Bethlehem town to Calvary
The Christ betook His way.
O'er roads that wound uphill and down
Our Lord went forth each day
Prepared to do His Father's work,
The plan of God Divine,
Nor matter cost or grief or pain,
"Thy will, O God, not mine."

From Bethlehem town to Calvary
The Christ still leads today.
In spirit and in truth He speaks
And hears us when we pray,
"Thy will, O God, not mine be done,
All glory be to Thee."
O let me walk that road of love
That leads to Calvary.

©

At Easter

Frieda Hawes

Now the golden hours of Easter
Come again across the land,
Bringing hope and faith and courage
And new strength to understand.

Hearts respond to warmth of springtime
With display of all things new,
So deep shadows can be lifted
To reveal a brighter view.

Then each life can find new purpose
In rebirth of all God's things
To inspire the golden moments
With the love that Easter brings!

©

The Message of Easter

Edwin C. Young

Imagine seeing at the break of day
A lonely figure walking your way.
He approached so stately, so friendly, so real,
He spoke words so sincere, they needed no seal;
His face worn with care was still most dear,
His voice so resonate, vibrant and clear,
He came to meet you with a warm kindly smile,
You knew He would walk with you the last long mile.

We walked together with much delight,
I would have walked with Him through the night,
But as in a dream He seemed to disappear,
Still He left a message so bold and clear.
His last words were, "I'm depending on you
To carry on the work, go forth and do."
The forces of evil are marching strong,
We must rise and trample out vice and wrong.

The Easter message of the risen Lord . . .
Go spread the word, be of one accord,
I am the truth, the light, the way,
Those who cometh, "I will not turn away."
For two thousand years this message of love
Has proven the truth of the Saviour above;
Time has not dimmed nor changed the word,
Still the greatest message the world has heard.

Easter brings a challenge to everyone
To carry on the work the Saviour's begun;
This is the plan of love and salvation,
To proclaim the message to every nation.
He gave His life, His all, the world to save,
And depends on us to be true and brave;
Let us answer the call with a ready will . . .
Go out and proclaim Him from hill to hill.

©

This is my commandment, That ye love one another, as I have loved you.

Greater love hath no man than this, that a man lay down his life for his friends.

Ye are my friends, if ye do whatever I command you.

Henceforth I call you not servants; for the servant knoweth not what his lord doeth: but I have called you friends; for all things that I have heard of my Father I have made known unto you.

ST. JOHN 15 : 12 - 15

The Night He Was Betrayed

Mrs. Russell Jones

Remember the prayer of Jesus
The night He was betrayed?
He poured out His soul to God,
But not because He was afraid.

His heart was heavy laden,
Bowed down with deep despair—
His eyes were filled with tears,
But no one seemed to care.

Then He heard the angry mob,
He saw their torches glare . . .
Judas betrayed Him with a kiss,
As He was standing there.

Pilate found no fault in Him,
But the multitude loudly cried,
"We do not believe He is the Christ,
Let Him be crucified."

They put on Him a scarlet robe,
Plaited thorns for His head—
They mocked, but He said nothing,
Then to Golgotha He was led.

©

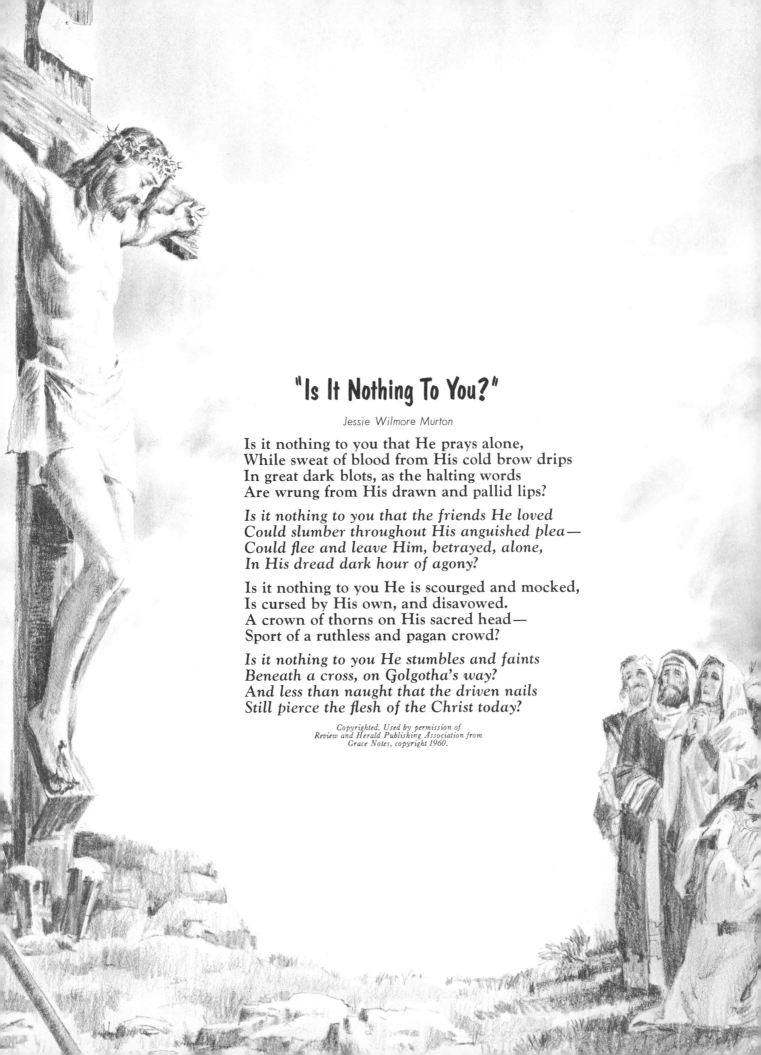

"Is It Nothing To You?"

Jessie Wilmore Murton

Is it nothing to you that He prays alone,
While sweat of blood from His cold brow drips
In great dark blots, as the halting words
Are wrung from His drawn and pallid lips?

*Is it nothing to you that the friends He loved
Could slumber throughout His anguished plea—
Could flee and leave Him, betrayed, alone,
In His dread dark hour of agony?*

Is it nothing to you He is scourged and mocked,
Is cursed by His own, and disavowed.
A crown of thorns on His sacred head—
Sport of a ruthless and pagan crowd?

*Is it nothing to you He stumbles and faints
Beneath a cross, on Golgotha's way?
And less than naught that the driven nails
Still pierce the flesh of the Christ today?*

Pilate said unto him, Art thou the King of the Jews?

Jesus answered, My kingdom is not of this world: if my kingdom were of this world, then would my servants fight, that I should not be delivered to the Jews: but now is my kingdom not from hence.

Pilate therefore said unto him, Art thou a king then?

Jesus answered, Thou sayest that I am a king. To this end was I born, and for this cause came I into the world, that I should bear witness unto the truth. Every one that is of the truth heareth my voice.

Pilate saith unto him, What is truth?

And when he had said this, he went out again unto the Jews, and saith unto them, I find in him no fault at all. Will ye therefore that I release unto you the King of the Jews?

Then cried they all again, saying, Not this man, but Barabbas. And Pilate saith unto them, Behold the man! Shall I crucify your King? The chief priests answered, We have no king but Caesar.

Pilate saith unto them, Take ye him, and crucify him.

From St. John 18 and 19

Painting Opposite
BEHOLD THE MAN
by John Walter

Borrowed

Author Unknown

They borrowed a bed to lay His head,
When Christ the Lord came down,
They borrowed a foal in the mountain pass
For Him to ride to town.
But the crown that He wore
And the cross that He bore
  Were His own.

He borrowed the bread when the crowd He fed
On the grassy mountainside;
He borrowed the dish of broken fish
With which He satisfied.
But the crown that He wore
And the cross that He bore
  Were His own.

He borrowed the ship in which to sit
To teach the multitude;
He borrowed the nest in which to rest,
He had never a home as rude.
But the crown that He wore
And the cross that He bore
  Were His own.

He borrowed a room on the way to the tomb,
The Passover lamb to eat.
They borrowed a cave, for Him a grave,
They borrowed a winding sheet.
But the crown that He wore
And the cross that He bore
  Were His own.

The thorns of His head were worn in my stead,
For me the Saviour died;
For guilt of my sin the nails drove in,
When Him they crucified.
Though the crown that He wore
And the cross that He bore
  Were His own . . .
They rightly were mine, instead.

Headlines of Long Ago

J. A. Greenlee

Jesus betrayed by one of His twelve,
Barabbas released in His stead;
The mob cried out, "Let us crucify Him . . ."
"No fault in this man," Pilate said.

They plaited His crown from the thorns of the field,
In scarlet He then was arrayed.
To Golgotha place they led Him away,
And His cross on Simon they laid.

Three crosses were raised on Calvary's hill,
Two thieves were crucified, too.
Jesus then prayed, "Father forgive,
For they know not what they do."

Darkness was spread all over the earth,
The veil of the temple was rent.
Joseph removed the body of Christ,
After Pilate had given consent.

In a tomb He was placed, from a rock it was hewn,
Where no one had lain before;
The sepulchre made sure, with the seal of the king,
And a guard was placed at the door.

An angel from heaven, the stone rolled away,
And Jesus came forth as He said;
The keepers with fear did tremble and shake
And acted as though they were dead.

On Damascus road He was seen by the two,
And again behind the closed door.
We rejoice in the fact that He arose from the dead,
And now is alive evermore.

©

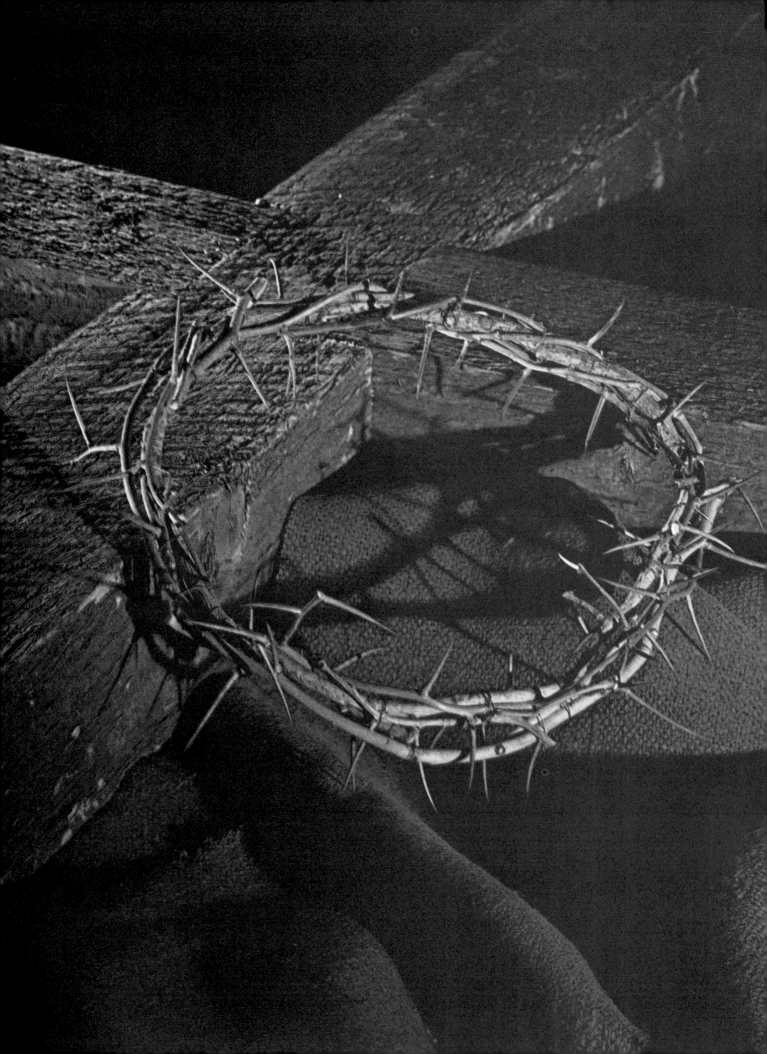

I Must Seek a Hill

Grace Noll Crowell

This is His night,
But oh, I cannot find Him in the crowd;
Its laughter is too loud;
Its voices are too raucous and too shrill.
I must turn back along old darkened ways
And seek a hill
Where winds are clean, and where the stars shine down
Clearer than they shine above a town.

This is His night.
The hill I seek is far and I must go
To find Him, for I know
That someway I shall come upon Him there,
The silver of the starshine on His face
And in His hair.
A look about Him, calm and still and white,
Will make me know Him on the hill tonight.

This is His night.
The glory of it clutches at my heart
And it is time to start.
He will be there and I shall call His name,
And through the starlight He will turn and speak
To one who came
A long, long way down darkened roads and dim,
To climb a high hill that she might find Him.

"He is Risen"

Author Unknown

How calm it is! Our eyes are cast afar upon a lonely hilltop, wet with dew, whence three lone crosses stand, now quiet, too, beneath the solitary morning star.

We wander to the lonely crypt once more, where three days since we laid our fallen Lord. We hoped to gain His kingdom by the sword. His body took our hopes behind that door.

But what is this? The stone is rolled away. An angel, clad in white, stands guardian there, and tells us "He is risen!"

Let us sing and make joyful in this glorious day! A golden sun is dawning bright and fair. 'Tis Easter morn! All hail our risen Lord and King!

"Because I Live"

Grace Noll Crowell

Christ said: "Because I live, ye shall live also."
O men, lay hold upon His blessed word.
This is our hope, like some high lifted banner
Unfurled against the sky. Our hearts have heard
No clearer message, and no truer music
Than this assurance, from the Christ's own tongue—
Because He lives, He says, we shall live also,
Forever joyous, forever young.

Forever to advance in greater knowledge,
To fully know the truth that sets us free,
To walk companioned by the living Saviour
Throughout the reaches of eternity—
Oh, what more blessed news could we be hearing
Than these words loosed upon the winds of time?
They lie ahead of us—the hills of heaven,
With Him for comrade, and with strength to climb!

I Wish

William Arnette Wofford

I wish I could have seen His face
All radiant that Easter morn . . .
A great light shining on His brow
That had been pierced by many a thorn.

I wish I could have seen His smile,
After the darkness and the gloom,
When Mary kissed His garment's hem
In wonder by the open tomb.

I wish I could have heard Him speak
There in the April garden when
He walked among the lilies and
Proclaimed eternal life for men.

But wishing is in vain, I know . . .
So I must be content to see
The miracle recurring in
Each blossomed bud and leaf and tree.

There is a warm assurance, too,
That of His love I am a part,
And that His resurrection lives
Forever in my heart.

©

The Easter Season

Virginia Katherine Oliver

When the Easter season comes
Our hearts are filled with glory
That is the true miracle
Of the wondrous Easter story.

As life anew comes to earth,
We understand in everything
Something of these sacred truths
In the beauty of each spring.

Life that long has been asleep
Like a peaceful spirit reborn,
Bursts into magnificence
To greet the joyous Easter morn.

Souls of men are lifted up
To planes above the commonplace
To blend with the eternal
Somewhere beyond in time and space.

©

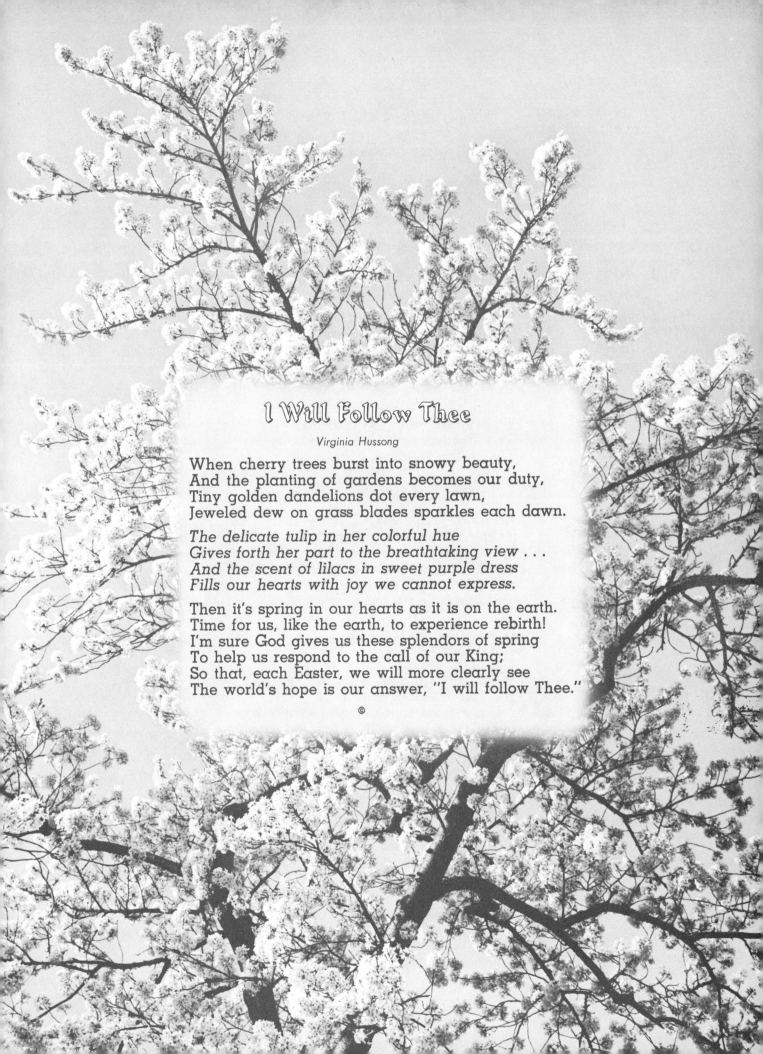

I Will Follow Thee

Virginia Hussong

When cherry trees burst into snowy beauty,
And the planting of gardens becomes our duty,
Tiny golden dandelions dot every lawn,
Jeweled dew on grass blades sparkles each dawn.

The delicate tulip in her colorful hue
Gives forth her part to the breathtaking view . . .
And the scent of lilacs in sweet purple dress
Fills our hearts with joy we cannot express.

Then it's spring in our hearts as it is on the earth.
Time for us, like the earth, to experience rebirth!
I'm sure God gives us these splendors of spring
To help us respond to the call of our King;
So that, each Easter, we will more clearly see
The world's hope is our answer, "I will follow Thee."

©

If Easter Be Not True

Henry H. Barstow, D.D.

If Easter be not true,
Then all the lilies low must lie;
The Flanders poppies fade and die;
The spring must lose her fairest bloom
For Christ were still within the tomb . . .
    If Easter be not true.

If Easter be not true,
Then faith must mount on broken wing;
Then hope no more immortal spring;
Then hope must lose her mighty urge;
Life prove a phantom, death a dirge . . .
    If Easter be not true.

If Easter be not true,
'Twere foolishness the cross to bear;
He dies in vain who suffered there;
What matter though we laugh or cry,
Be good or evil, live or die,
    If Easter be not true?

If Easter be not true . . .
But it is true, and Christ is risen!
And mortal spirit from its prison
Of sin and death with Him may rise!
Worthwhile the struggle, sure the prize,
    Since Easter, aye, is true!

Our sincere thanks to the author whose address we were unable to locate.

So Many Hearts Are Brave

Grace Noll Crowell

So many hearts are brave. Each day I see
The lifted banners of their courage shine
Out of the myriad eyes that look in mine.

The banners mankind carry as they march
To prove that they are undefeated still
Though tired feet must often drag behind;
Though there be scarcely strength to climb the hill.

Brave women, and brave men, who go their way
Without the blare of music down the street;
Without the cheers, or the encouragement
Of words that would be heartening and sweet.

So many have the courage to go on
Undaunted by their loss, or pain or fear;
Beaten perhaps, yet holding in their souls
The beautiful bright quality of cheer.

So many hearts are brave though well they know
How rough the road is that their feet must go.

I saw Him there
   where mountains brushed
   the sky.

I saw Him there
   where trees and grass grace
   the dawn.

I saw Him there
   where rippling brooks don
   the green.

I saw Him there
   where waving flowers toss
   and speak.

I saw Him there
   where eyes of man reflect
   His peace within.

Julia A. Martin

©

Sunrise

George L. Ehrman

Very early in the morning
At the rising of the sun,
They came and saw the stone
   was rolled away . . .
An angel in the sepulchre
Spoke to each and everyone,
"Behold the place where once
   your Saviour lay."

They went out from the place of night
Into a garden filled with light
   And found our Saviour there . . .
They found Him on a lonely road,
They found Him where each one abode,
   For He was everywhere!

Very early here this morning
At the rising of the sun,
We come because the stone
   was rolled away . . .
Each, a bearer of glad tidings,
Witnessing to everyone,
"He lives within my heart
   this Easter Day!"

©

Christ Is Risen

Grace Noll Crowell

Often through life we have our own
   dark garden:
Our own Gethsemane,
With no hint at all of an early
   springtime morning,
Silvering bush and tree.
Then suddenly a startling cry
   is lifting
To meet our desperate need . . .
The words ring crystal-clear:
   "Christ is risen !"
And Christ is risen indeed.

We see the stone rolled from the
   darkened cavern,
An angel, clothed in white,
Has been sent down from heaven by
   the Father
To give new hope, new light
To all who sorrow, and our
   weeping ceases.
We are no longer sad . . .
The greatest news broadcast
   throughout the ages
Has made us glad.
Christ is risen, the blessed
   Christ is risen.
Cry it aloud. Oh, emphasize
   each word!
Lift as one voice a hallelujah chorus
Until the last lone seeking
   heart has heard.

The Glorious Dawn

Ella E. Doxsee

Gone is the fear that has held us in bondage
As we think of that first Easter Day,
The glorious dawn after earth's darkest night,
And the tomb with the stone rolled away.

Angels came down from heaven that day
To roll the great stone from the tomb,
To tell to man that Christ lived once again,
And to rob the grave of its fear and its gloom.

The promise of life eternal is ours...
For this we rejoice on this glad Easter Day,
For the Lord of all hath conquered the grave
And the stone has been rolled forever away.

©

The Valley Church

Elma Rowbotham

The valley church is yours and mine,
It has an open door,
Green-robed mountains are the walls
And valley grass its floor.
The roof is but a sweep of sky
Illumined by the sun
Or, when night shades the vale, the stars,
Appearing one and one.
The altar is a dogwood tree,
We kneel before such grace;
An altar cloth so chaste and white
The lilies at its base.
The valley church has sanctity
For here have angels trod,
Here we may worship and behold
The Presence of our God.

©

I was glad when they said unto me, Let us go into the house of the LORD.

PSALM 122:1

PAUL MANN

Benediction

Marian L. Moore

Upon the stillness of the air
I heard the clear tones of a bell
Ring out a song across the land;
I heard an echo rise and swell.

And there against the sunset sky
A cross set forth in dark relief . . .
The symbol of a risen Christ,
All faith and hope and staunch belief.

The bell-notes sweet upon the breeze,
(How near the cross is to a star,)
The gentle hand of God's great love . . .
A benediction from afar.

©